Super STEM Activities

Amazing Activities with LIGHT and COLOR

Anne O'Daly

Published in 2023 by Enslow Publishing, LLC
29 East 21st Street, New York, NY 10010

Design Manager: Keith Davis
Design and Illustration: squareandcircus.co.uk

Manufactured in the United States of America

CPSIA compliance information: Batch #CSENS23: For further information contact Enslow Publishing LLC, New York, New York at 1-800-398-2504.

Cataloging-in-Publication Data

Names: O'Daly, Anne.
Title: Amazing activities with light and color / Anne O'Daly.
Description: New York : Enslow Publishing, 2023. | Series: Super STEM Activities | Includes glossary and index.
Identifiers: ISBN 9781978529786 (pbk.) | ISBN 9781978529809 (library bound) | ISBN 9781978529793 (6pack) | ISBN 9781978529816 (ebook)
Subjects: LCSH: Light--Experiments--Juvenile literature. | Color--Experiments--Juvenile literature.
Classification: LCC QC360 O339 2023 | DDC 535.078--dc23

CONTENTS

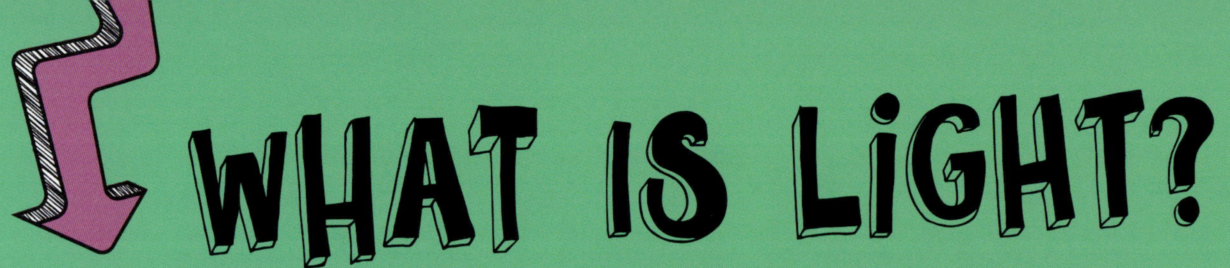

WHAT IS LIGHT?

Light is a kind of energy. Nearly all light comes from the Sun and other stars in the universe. But light comes from other sources, too, such as light bulbs and candles.

Particle or wave?

For a long time, scientists couldn't agree about what light is. Some said it moved as a wave. Others thought light was a stream of tiny particles. Early in the twentieth century, Albert Einstein (1879–1955) showed that light is made up of tiny particles called photons. These particles move as waves. Both ideas were true!

Most of this book follows a branch of science called optics. This considers light as waves. Waves of light behave like other waves, such as water waves or sound waves.

RAINBOW COLORS

Light looks white, but it is a mixture of different colors. This range of colors is called the spectrum. Light has colors because it travels in waves. Red light has the longest wavelength. Violet has the shortest wavelength.

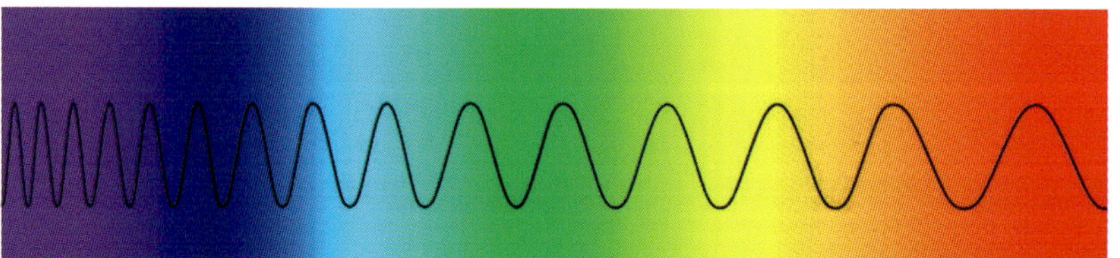

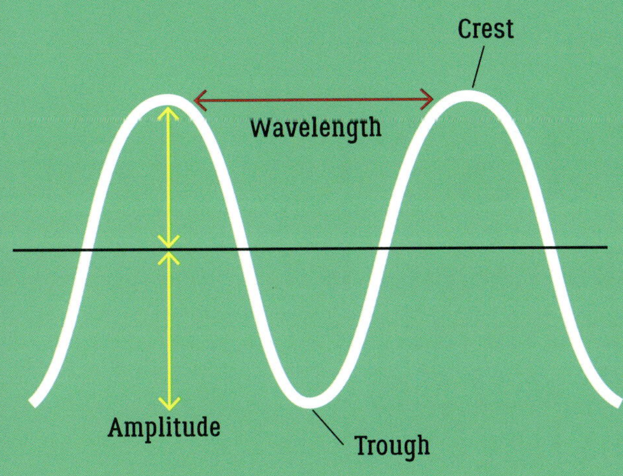

Light waves

Waves move up and down as they travel. The highest point of a wave is its crest. The lowest point is the trough. The distance between two crests or two troughs is the wavelength. Amplitude is the height of a crest or the depth of a trough.

When waves meet, they create interference. Sometimes crests combine to make waves that have twice the amplitude. At other times, the crest and trough cancel each other out.

Reflections

When light hits a surface, it bounces back. Some surfaces make light rays bounce off in one direction, which makes an image. Others make light rays bounce off in all directions, which makes the surface look dull. Objects look colored because of the way they reflect light. White objects reflect all the colors. Red objects reflect red light but absorb other colors. Black objects absorb all the colors.

THINK LIKE A SCIENTIST!

The best way to learn about science is to do experiments. Scientists use the scientific method to guide what they do. This is a series of questions that help them work in a logical way.

1. Ask a question—this might be based on something you've seen (observed) or on something you've read.

2. Come up with a hypothesis. This is your best guess or prediction for what might happen.

3. Test your hypothesis with an experiment.

4. Write down the results. Did they show what you thought they would?

5. Share the results with other people and ask them to repeat your experiment.

Spreading out

Light waves spread out, or diffract, when they move through a very narrow space. If there are several spaces for the light to pass through, the diffracted light waves combine and interference happens. The interference shows as patterns of colors.

Bending light

When you look at a straw in a glass of water, it seems to bend where it meets the water. When light moves from one substance to another, its speed changes and it changes direction slightly. Light refracts, or bends, when it moves from one substance to another. When light moves from air to water it slows down.

GET READY

All of the experiments in this book are about light and color. You can do them in any order. Before you start, check that you have all the items you need. Most of the supplies can be found at home, but you might have to get some from a store. Make sure that you have enough space to carry out the experiment. Check with an adult before you start—some of the experiments might get a bit messy! Also ask an adult for help with anything that uses sharp tools or flames. Most of all, have fun!

TWO-WAY MIRROR

Can a mirror work on both sides?
Follow these steps to find out.
And join your face with someone else's!

WHAT YOU NEED:

- 12-inch (30 cm) square piece of glass
- 12-inch (30 cm) square sheet of Mylar to cover the glass (ask for antiglare window film in a hardware store)
- cloth tape
- 2 electric lamps
- modeling clay
- an assistant

1. Cover one side of the glass with the sheet of Mylar film. Make sure the film is smooth and flat against the glass.

2. Use strips of cloth tape to stick the film to the edge of the glass. Cover the sharp edges of the glass using more tape.

STEM CONCEPTS:
reflection, light waves

TIPS:

- TRY NOT TO SHINE YOUR LAMP DIRECTLY INTO THE OTHER PERSON'S EYES.
- COVER THE EDGES OF THE GLASS TO AVOID ACCIDENTAL CUTS.

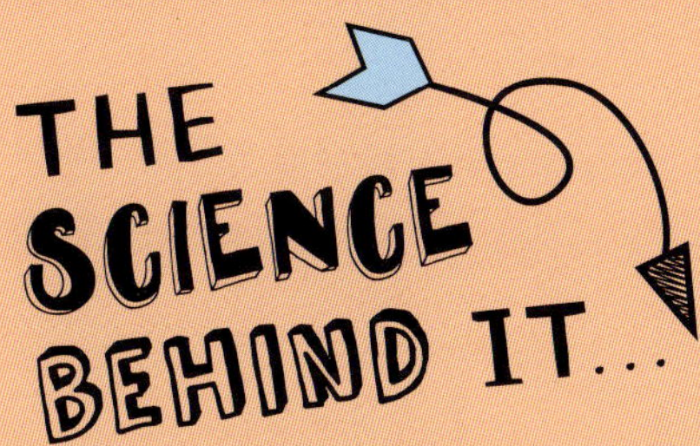

THE SCIENCE BEHIND IT...

You saw a reflection of your face when your lamp was switched on. When your friend's light was off, very little light passed through the mirror from the other side. Nearly all the light you saw in the mirror was reflected from your own side.

3. Put balls of modeling clay on a table. Push the mirror into the clay so that it stands upright. Make sure it is steady before you let go.

4. Stand one lamp on each side of the mirror. Ask your assistant to sit on one side of the mirror. Close the drapes and turn out the lights. Sit facing your assistant on the other side of the mirror. Take turns switching on the lamps to illuminate your faces while you look at the mirror. Try turning on one light at a time. Then try with both lights on at the same time.

RAINBOW PATTERNS

Do this experiment to split white light and make a beautiful, shimmering rainbow.

WHAT YOU NEED:

- two 12-inch (30 cm) squares of Plexiglas about 1/8 inch (3 mm) thick
- soap and water
- clean cloth
- tape
- scissors
- piece of dark paper 12 inches (30 cm) square
- desk lamp

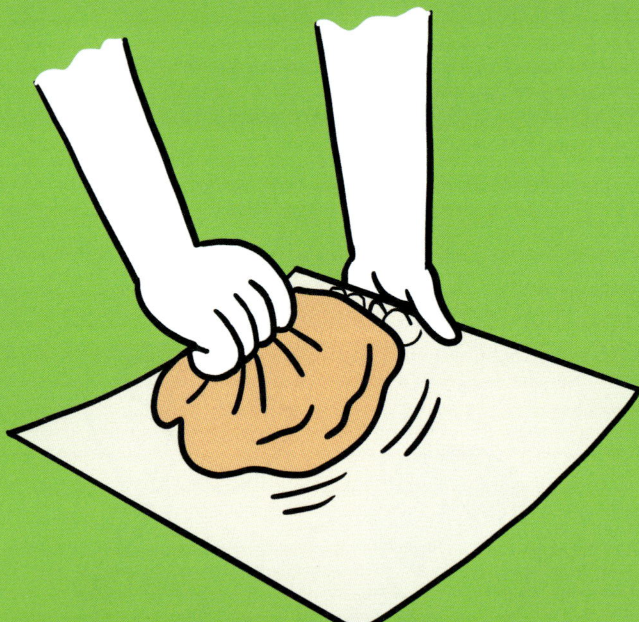

1. Wash both sides of the Plexiglas squares with soap and water. Rinse with fresh water, then dry the surfaces with a clean cloth.

STEM CONCEPTS:

reflection, interference

2. Put both squares of Plexiglas together. Put tape around the edges to hold them tightly in place.

3. Tape the square of dark paper over one side of the Plexiglas sheets.

4. Hold the Plexiglas "sandwich" under a bright desk lamp with the papered side facing downward.

5. Patterns of different colors should appear in the Plexiglas. These are caused by light waves interfering with each other. Gently bend the Plexiglas and notice how the patterns change.

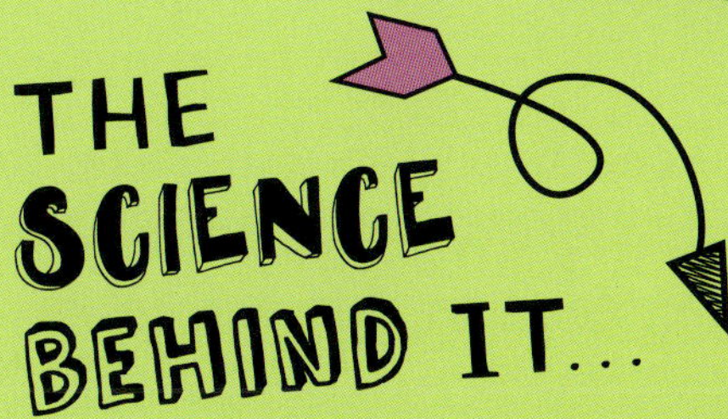

THE SCIENCE BEHIND IT...

Light from the lamp reflected off the bottom of the first sheet and the top of the second sheet of Plexiglas. The reflected light waves interfered with each other and made a rainbow. Bending the Plexiglas changed the space between the sheets. This altered the patterns.

FISHBOWL LENS

People use lenses in telescopes, binoculars, and pairs of eyeglasses. But did you know that water can act as a lens?

WHAT YOU NEED:

- round glass bowl
- water
- candle
- dish
- piece of thick white cardboard
- ruler
- newspaper

1. Fill the glass bowl with water. This will be the lens.

2. Put the candle on the dish. Place the dish 12 inches (30 cm) from the bowl of water. Ask an adult to light the candle.

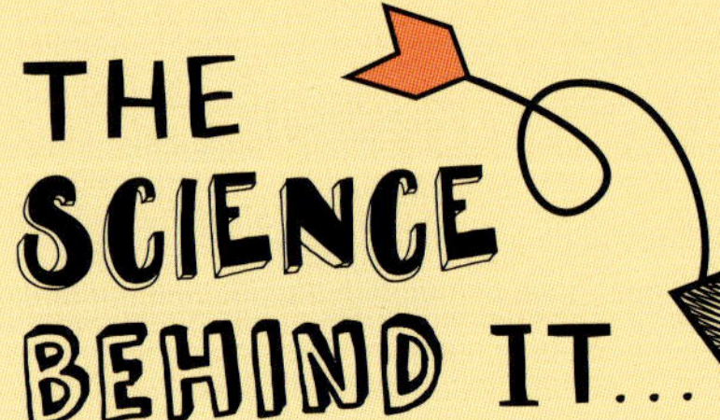

The bowl of water was like a lens. Light from the candle bent as it went through the bowl. It bent again as it entered the water. When the light passed into the air on the other side, it refracted again but in the opposite direction. That's why the image on the cardboard was upside down.

3. Hold the cardboard up on the other side of the bowl.

4. Slowly move the cardboard away from the bowl. Stop when you see an image of the candle flame on the cardboard. How does this image compare to the real flame?

STEM CONCEPTS:
refraction, lenses, light waves

TIPS:

- INSTEAD OF LOOKING AT THE CANDLE FLAME, TRY HOLDING A PIECE OF NEWSPAPER UP BEHIND THE BOWL OF WATER. DO THE WORDS LOOK BIGGER?

SLOW DOWN LIGHT

Does light travel at different speeds through different objects? Try this experiment to find out.

WHAT YOU NEED:

- 2 glasses
- jug of water
- cooking oil
- baby oil
- 2 clear glass stirrers, such as cocktail stirrers

1. Pour water into one of the glasses until it is half full.

2. Slowly pour a thick layer of cooking oil on top of the water.

3. Half-fill the second glass with baby oil.

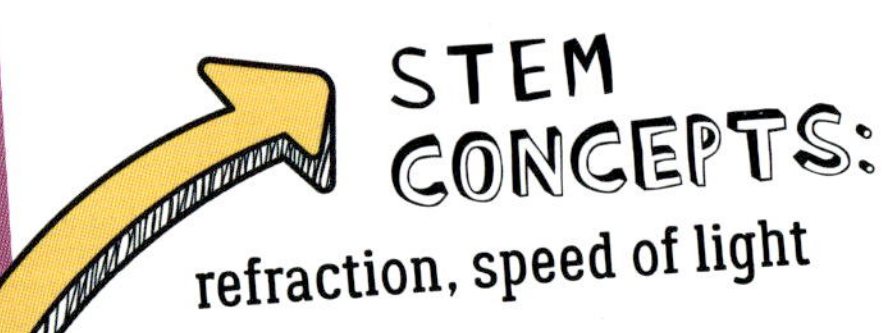

STEM CONCEPTS:
refraction, speed of light

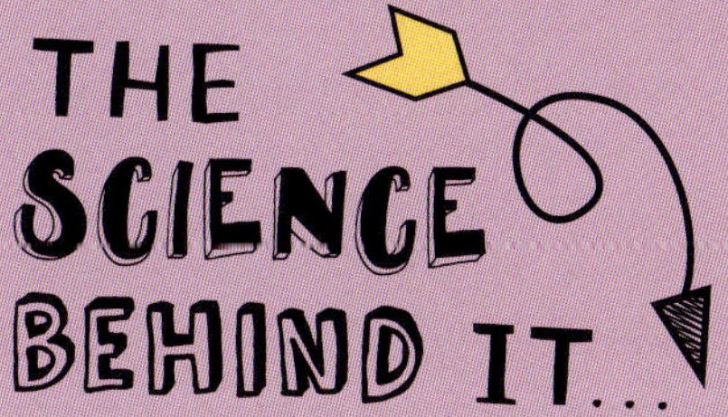

The stirrer became faint, or even disappeared, where it passed through the cooking oil. The stirrer in the baby oil should have been easier to see. The light bends most as it passes into and out of the stirrer in air. It bends a bit less when the stirrer is in water. The stirrers are hardest to see in the oils because light bends relatively little when it passes through oil. This makes the stirrers look faint.

4. Put a clear glass stirrer in each glass. What can you see when you look at the glasses from the side? Are some parts of the stirrers fainter than other parts?

MAKE A TELESCOPE

Telescopes collect light from stars millions of miles away. They use lenses to make the images big enough to see.

WHAT YOU NEED:

- glass or plastic lenses
- 2 cardboard tubes (one slightly narrower than the other so it will just fit inside the larger one)
- tape

1. Choose two lenses that work together to focus on an object. To do this, hold a small lens near your eye. Hold a larger lens farther away. Look through them at an object. Move the larger lens until the object is in focus. Your cardboard tubes need to be as long as the distance between the lenses.

! NEVER USE A TELESCOPE TO LOOK DIRECTLY AT THE SUN OR ANY BRIGHT LIGHTS. YOU COULD SERIOUSLY DAMAGE YOUR EYES AND IT MAY EVEN BLIND YOU.

STEM CONCEPTS: lenses, focal length, focus

2. Rest the larger lens on one end of the large cardboard tube. Put a strip of tape around the end of the tube. Press it down gently over the edge of the lens to hold it in place.

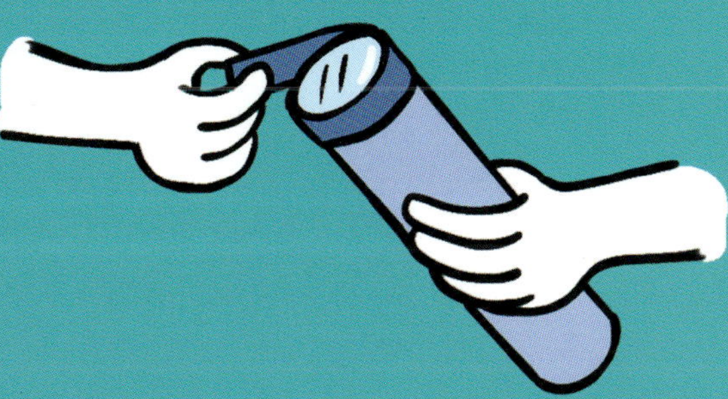

3. Put the smaller lens on the end of the narrower tube. Tape it in place.

4. Slide the open end of the smaller tube into the open end of the large tube. Look at an object at a distance. Bring it into focus by moving the small tube in and out of the larger tube.

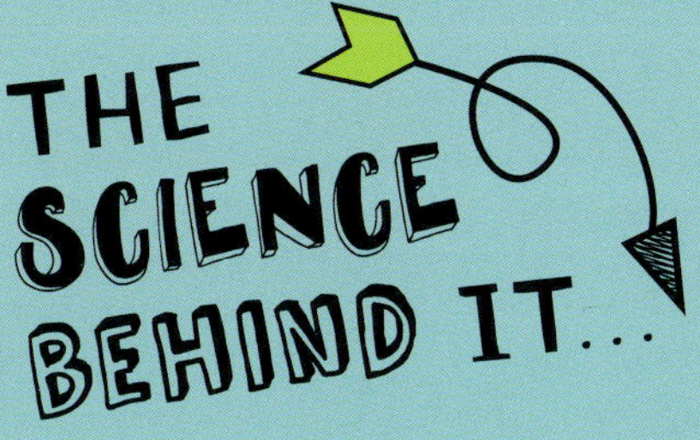

The length between the outer lens and your eyes is the telescope's focal length. This is the distance the large lens needed to focus light from the object through the small lens onto your eye. The small lens magnified the light image so that your eye could see the object clearly.

TRAPPING LIGHT

Sometimes light gets trapped inside a material. Follow these steps to find out how this happens.

WHAT YOU NEED:

- a glass tank full of water
- milk
- bright flashlight with a narrow beam
- washable felt-tip pen
- protractor
- an assistant
- ruler

1. Clean the tank and fill it with water. Add a tiny amount of milk. You should still be able to see through the water. Close the drapes and turn out the lights.

2. Hold the flashlight at the side of the tank. Shine the light beam through the side of the tank. Angle the beam upward so that it hits the water surface from below.

3. Move the angle of the flashlight so that the beam hits the surface at different angles. Can you find the critical angle? That is when the light travels along the surface of the water.

STEM CONCEPTS:
reflection, critical angle

4. When you have found the critical angle, use the felt-tip pen to mark crosses on the outside of the tank to mark the path of the light beam.

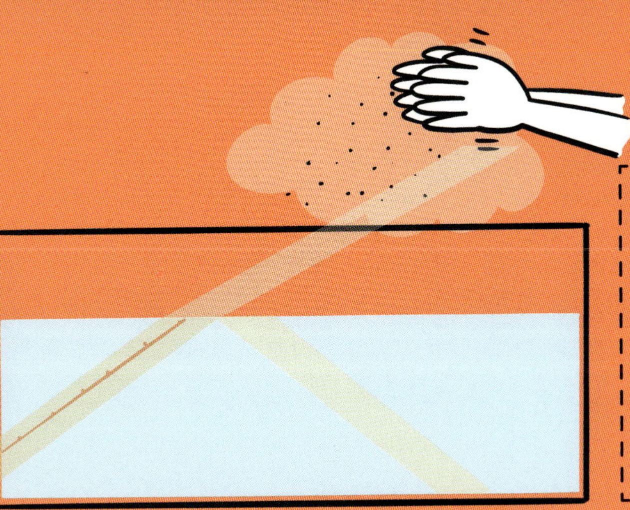

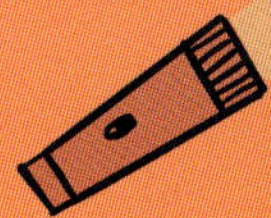

TIPS:

- YOU COULD SPRINKLE SOME TALCUM POWDER ABOVE THE TANK TO MAKE THE EMERGING BEAM SHOW UP.

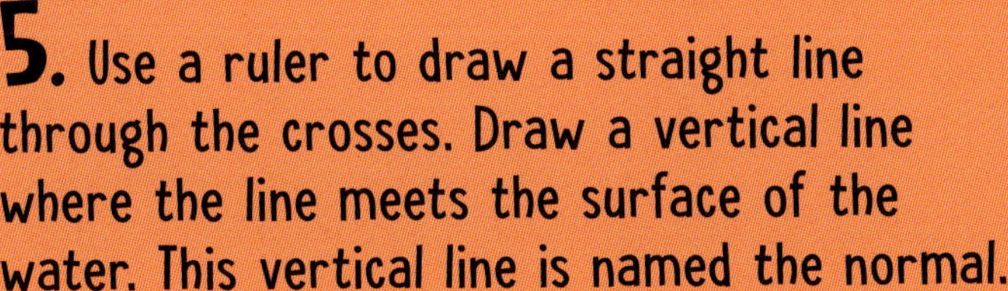

5. Use a ruler to draw a straight line through the crosses. Draw a vertical line where the line meets the surface of the water. This vertical line is named the normal.

6. Use the protractor to measure the angle between the two lines. It is the critical angle for water.

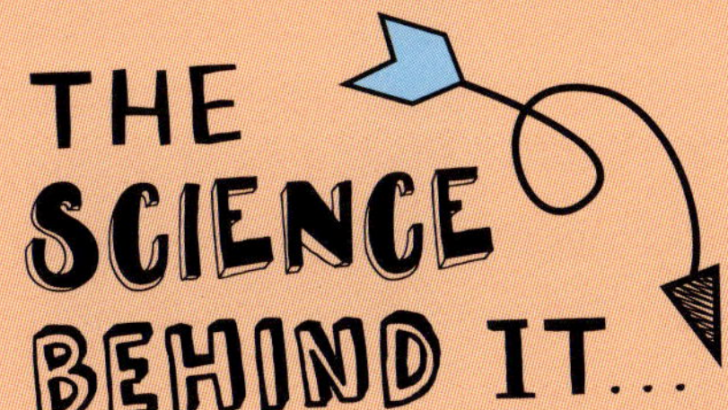

The angle between the vertical line and the sloping line should be about 49°. This is called the critical angle. When the angle of incidence (the angle at which light hits the water) is greater than the critical angle, the light reflects off the water instead of passing through. It bounces back and gets trapped under the water.

PINHOLE CAMERA

A pinhole camera is a simple camera without a lens. Follow these steps to make one, and try making images appear on a screen.

WHAT YOU NEED:

- shoebox
- paintbrush
- black paint
- newspaper
- scissors
- tape
- tracing paper
- aluminum foil
- pin

1. Paint the inside of the box black, including the lid.

2. Cut a small square out of both ends of the box.

THE SCIENCE BEHIND IT...

Light shines into the box through the tiny opening. Because light travels in a straight line, light from above the hole reaches the inside of the box below the hole. Light from below the hole reaches the inside of the box above the hole. This makes the image display upside down.

3. Cover one hole with aluminum foil. Keep the foil tight, and tape around the edges so that no light can get into the box.

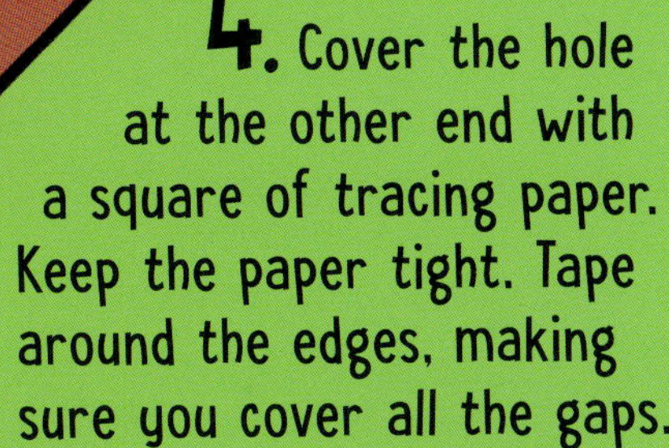

4. Cover the hole at the other end with a square of tracing paper. Keep the paper tight. Tape around the edges, making sure you cover all the gaps.

STEM CONCEPTS:
light waves travel in straight lines

5. Put the lid on the box. If the lid is loose, tape around the edges to hold it in place. Cover all the gaps. Make a tiny hole in the center of the foil using a pin. You now have a pinhole camera!

6. Point the foil end at something and look at the image that forms on the screen.

SPECTROMETER

Scientists use a spectrometer to split light into its different wavelengths. Follow these steps to make your own.

WHAT YOU NEED:

- shoebox
- scissors
- tape
- construction paper
- thin mesh window screen
- lens
- flashlight
- book
- white paper
- modeling clay
- colored pencils

1. Cut a 2-inch (5 cm) square hole in each end of the shoebox. Tape two pieces of construction paper over the hole at one end so that the pieces almost touch. Leave a narrow vertical slit between them to let light into the box.

2. Cut three pieces of mesh window screen to fit over the hole in the other end of the box. Overlap the pieces and tape them in place.

STEM CONCEPTS:
light, wavelength, spectrum

3. Put the lid on the box. If it is not a very tight fit, tape around the edges so the light can't get in. You now have a spectrometer! Shine a flashlight into the slit and hold the lens in front of the mesh at the other end. Put the white paper on the table on the other side of the lens. A spectrum should appear on it.

4. Use a blob of clay to hold the lens in place. Use your colored pencils to copy the spectrum onto the white paper.

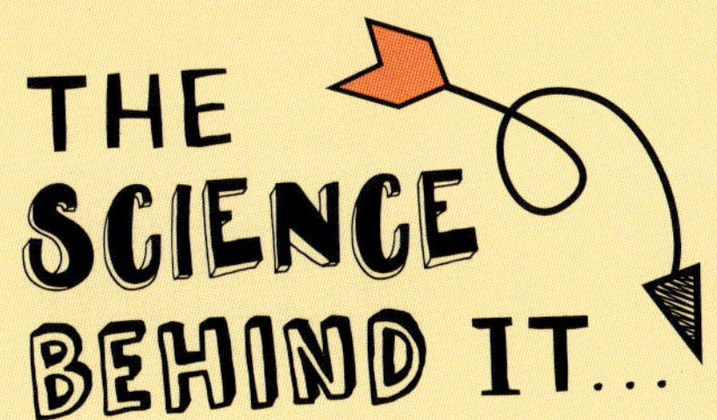

The lid on the box kept out light from all sources except the flashlight. Light from the flashlight was diffracted by the slit and the mesh, and the spaces were small enough to spread the different wavelengths of light into a spectrum.

MOIRÉ PATTERNS

Find out what happens when light waves interfere, and make some beautiful swirling patterns.

WHAT YOU NEED:

- two small combs
- thin pen
- paper
- ruler
- access to a photocopier and transparencies
- thin mesh window screen

1. Hold the combs up in front of a light source, such as a table lamp. Slowly move the teeth of one comb in front of the teeth of the other. Can you see patterns of lines?

STEM CONCEPTS:

light waves, interference, diffraction

2. Draw some parallel lines or a pattern of concentric circles (circles inside each other) on a piece of white paper. Photocopy the pattern onto two transparencies. Overlap them to make moiré patterns.

3. Slide two pieces of mesh window screen over each other. Can you see moiré patterns within them?

THE SCIENCE BEHIND IT...

When light shines through a narrow opening, it spreads out (diffracts). If there are two slits close together, the light waves spreading out from the slits interfere with each other. Moiré patterns are caused by interference. When the combs passed each other, their teeth lined up, then didn't line up, and then lined up again. When the combs didn't line up, a pattern appeared. At first it had dark lines packed together, but then they spread out.

TIPS:

- DO NOT USE THE SUN AS A LIGHT SOURCE IN THIS EXPERIMENT. LOOKING DIRECTLY AT THE SUN WILL DAMAGE YOUR EYES.

SUNSET IN A GLASS

What makes the sky blue, sunsets red, and clouds white? The answer is scattering. You can investigate this with a flashlight and a glass of milky water.

WHAT YOU NEED:

- a large glass
- water
- milk
- powerful flashlight
- plastic sheets of different colors

1. Fill the glass with water, then add a little milk.

2. Shine the flashlight through the glass. Look at the beam of light through the glass from the opposite side. Then look through the glass on the same side as the flashlight, and from halfway around.

3. Hold a colored plastic sheet between the flashlight and the glass. Shine the flashlight through the plastic sheet. Look all around the glass again. Does the beam of light look any different?

STEM CONCEPTS: light scattering

THE SCIENCE BEHIND IT...

The milky water scattered light as the atmosphere does. The water was slightly blue near the beam on the same side as the flashlight. From the other side, it looked red. Blue light is scattered most easily, so water near the flashlight turns blue. The colored sheets turned the light beam into one color. The milk scatters the light as before, but the color should look the same from any direction.

4. Try the experiment again using different-colored sheets of plastic. Write down what you see with each color.

SEPARATING COLORS

How many colors are in a marker? Try this experiment to find out how to separate colors.

WHAT YOU NEED:
- white paper towel
- scissors
- measuring cup
- glass beaker or cup
- water
- 2 washable felt-tip markers of different colors
- clothespin

1. Cut a piece of paper towel about 4 inches (10 cm) long and 1 inch (2.5 cm) wide.

2. Pour about 1 inch (2.5 cm) of water from the measuring cup into the glass beaker or cup.

STEM CONCEPTS:
molecules, chromatography

3. Using the felt-tip pens, draw two dots of different colors about 2 inches (5 cm) from the end of the paper strip. The dots should be about the same size.

4. Attach the strip of paper towel to the edge of the beaker using a clothespin. The end with the two dots should just be touching the water.

5. As the water gradually moves up the paper strip, it will take the chemicals that make up the colors of each dot with it. You will be surprised by the colors that appear!

THE SCIENCE BEHIND IT...

Most colors, like those in markers, are made up of different-colored dyes mixed together. Some are heavier, some are lighter. The dyes in washable markers dissolve in water. When water reached the spots of color, it dissolved the dyes and carried them up the paper. The dyes with larger molecules separate out first and move more slowly. The lighter dyes move faster and further up the paper. The technique you used is called chromatography. Scientists use it to separate substances into their parts.

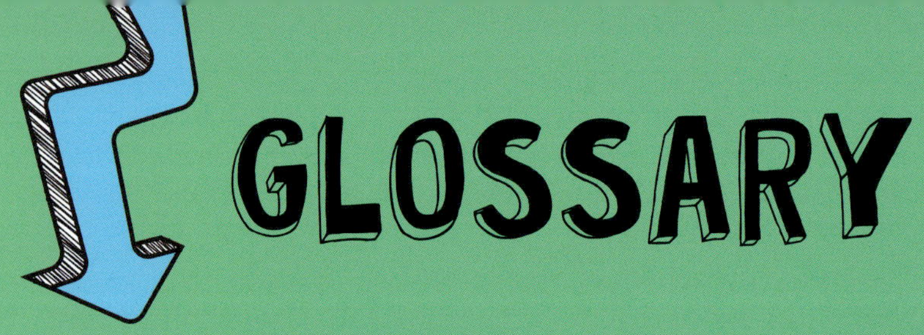

Amplitude the height of a wave's crest or the depth of its trough

Atmosphere the layers of gas that surround a planet

Crest the top of a wave

Critical angle the angle above which refraction happens

Diffraction spreading out in waves

Focal length the distance from a lens where light rays come together and form an image

Focus where light rays meet and form an image after traveling through a lens

Interference the way light beams change when they meet

Lens a transparent object that bends light; found in telescopes and eyeglasses

Moiré patterns swirling patterns that seem to appear behind overlapping, repeating sets of lines and dots

Optics the area of science that studies light behaving as a wave

Reflect describes the way light "bounces" back off the surface of water, glass, metal, and so on

Refract describes the way light rays bend when they pass from one kind of material (such as water) to another (such as air)

Spectrometer an instrument that diffracts light to make a spectrum

Spectrum the range of colors that make up white light

Telescope an instrument that uses lenses to magnify images of distant objects

Trough the lowest part of a wave

Wavelength the distance between two neighboring crests or two neighboring troughs of a wave

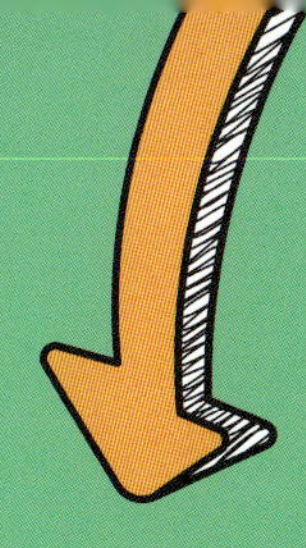

FURTHER RESOURCES

BOOKS

Abud, Gary Jr. **What Color Will It Be? (Science with Scarlett).** Covenant Books, 2019

Gardner, Robert. **A Kid's Book of Experiments with Color (Surprising Science).** Enslow Publishing, 2016

Mould, Steve. **Science Is Magic.** DK Penguin Random House, 2019

WEBSITES

www.optics4kids.org/activities
Visit this website for activities and projects.

www.sciencekids.co.nz/light.html
This website has facts, information, and quizzes about light.

www.fizzicseducation.com.au/category/150-science-experiments/light-sound-experiments/
Try the experiments on this website to discover more about light.

Publisher's note to educators and parents: Our editors have carefully reviewed these websites to ensure that they are suitable for students. Many websites change frequently, however, and we cannot guarantee that a site's future contents will continue to meet our high standards of quality and educational value. Be advised that students should be closely supervised whenever they access the internet.

INDEX